SLIMMING WO

LOW-FAT
cooking

D0519029

WH S

This edition first published in Great Britain in 2002 by Ebury Press
for WHSmith, Greenbridge Road, Swindon SN3 3LD

1 3 5 7 9 10 8 6 4 2

Text © Slimming World 2002
Food photography © Ebury Press 2002

Ebury Press
Random House, 20 Vauxhall Bridge Road, London SW1V 2SA

Random House Australia (Pty) Limited
20 Alfred Street, Milsons Point, Sydney, New South Wales 2061, Australia

Random House New Zealand Limited
18 Poland Road, Glenfield, Auckland 10, New Zealand

Random House South Africa (Pty) Limited
Endulini, 5A Jubilee Road, Parktown 2193, South Africa

The Random House Group Limited Reg. No. 954009

www.randomhouse.co.uk

A CIP catalogue record for this book is available from the British Library.

Editor: Gillian Haslam
Designer: Christine Wood
Photographer: Craig Robertson
Food Stylist: Jules Beresford
Stylist: Helen Trent

ISBN 009188411X

Papers used by Ebury Press are natural, recyclable products made from wood grown in
sustainable forests.

Printed and bound in Italy by GraphicomSrl

CONTENTS

Title page: Salmon and Asparagus Salad, page 68

Above: Strawberry and Raspberry Filo Slices, page 90

INTRODUCTION

There are plenty of 'healthy eating' cookery books about these days, so what is it that makes these Slimming World recipes special? The answer is that they've been devised using Slimming World's unique Food Optimising system, which helps hundreds of thousands of people every year to discover a way of enjoying food and losing weight that's different from any other 'diet'.

When you try these dishes, you can be assured that you will be eating in the way that is recognised as being the healthiest for people wanting to lose weight today. That's because Food Optimising has been developed in line with the latest mainstream scientific thinking on nutrition – there's nothing faddy or cranky about it.

All the experts agree that to lose weight, you have to change your 'energy balance', so that you are expending more energy than you take in. With most weight loss plans, this means endless weighing, measuring and counting – of calories, fat grams, or some other kind of unit. Most of us have had a run-in with this kind of diet at some point during our search for a slimmer shape – and most of us hated it. Food Optimising, however, can bring about a revolution in your eating habits and weight loss. The recipes work because they help you learn how to satisfy your appetite by making healthy food choices that limit your energy intake quite naturally. This doesn't mean eating less! Many people following the Food Optimising plan find that they are eating even more than before, and losing weight incredibly successfully.

When you try these recipes you'll be amazed how full your plate will be. It's what it is filled with that counts. And the best aspect of Food Optimising is that you choose what kind of meals suit you most. Each day you can follow either a Green or Original menu. Green menus are ideal if you love filling up on unlimited amounts of pasta, rice, potatoes and tasty vegetable dishes like curries and chillis. Original menus will suit you if a full English breakfast, mixed grill, roast beef, fish and seafood are your idea of heaven. And on both Green and Original days, you'll find there is a huge variety of Free Foods – delicious, satisfying foods that you can eat as much of as you like.

Stir-Fried Summer
Vegetables, page 66

The science behind Food Optimising is based on understanding why certain foods help produce signals that stop us wanting to eat when our body doesn't need any more and which foods stimulate the triggers that prevent us from eating again until our body requires more energy. Proteins, carbohydrates and fibre, all of which are incorporated into the Food Optimising system, all help to regulate our appetite in different ways. Fat, sugar and non-filling but calorie-laden elements in our food fill us up for a much shorter time. Fat is energy dense. It has more than twice as many calories per gram as carbohydrates and protein. You eat a lot more calories from fat before you feel full than you do when you eat carbohydrate or protein. So, the amount of fat in your meal can affect the total amount of calories you eat in that same meal. Protein fills you effectively as you eat and helps you feel full for longer, just as carbohydrates do. So basing your meals around protein-rich foods will help you not to overeat. Complex carbohydrates such as pasta and potatoes are much bulkier than refined carbohydrates like sugar and can help you feel fuller. They usually contain plenty of fibre and this adds bulk. Fibre slows both the digestion and absorption of food and gives us a more gradual release of sugar into the bloodstream as the carbohydrate you've eaten breaks down – and this helps suppress appetite for longer.

The results of all of this for slimmers are brilliantly simple: what you'll find when using these recipes is that you'll feel full more quickly and that that feeling of fullness lasts hours longer.

The other big difference you'll find with these Slimming World dishes is that you won't believe that you're on a diet, and neither will anyone else. They're so tasty, filling and healthy that the whole family will enjoy them – so no more preparing separate meals because you're slimming. The recipes are ideal for entertaining, too.

ARE YOU READY TO START ?

Food that's filling and slimming – that's what this book is all about! The most satisfying and nutritious meals to help you lose weight, without ever having to think about calories again. The following menus and recipes will help you to get started and we know you'll enjoy the variety and the feeling of losing weight comfortably. Here are some tips to ensure success:

- Be realistic – it's easier to keep up gradual and small changes to your eating habits than making major changes.

- Set yourself mini-targets, such as 1.5 kg (3 lb), then 4 kg (half a stone), etc. Reward yourself when you reach your mini-target with a treat such as a special day out or a new outfit.

- Set goals that mean something to you personally, such as being able to play football with the children, dropping a dress size, or feeling confident enough to go swimming.

- Use lots of flavourings such as fresh herbs, garlic, lemon juice, chilli and Worcestershire sauce to add variety and get your taste-buds tingling.

- Make a list of the reasons why you want to slim and what you look forward to when you've lost weight. Keep it handy and look at it whenever your motivation flags.

- Always include your favourite foods as part of your healthy balanced diet. If you ban foods, you are likely to feel deprived and then 'rebel'.

- We all have days when our good intentions disappear! Overdoing it on one day won't jeopardise your weight loss in the long term. Enjoy it without feeling guilty and start again the next day.

- Aim to add some extra activity into your daily routine. 'Exercise' needn't mean formal gym sessions: climbing stairs, walking and gardening all count. It's more important to start slowly and keep up with whatever activity you have chosen than to 'go for the burn'. And do check with your GP before starting.

- Support could make a crucial difference to your success. Tell chosen trusted friends or family that you're trying to slim and that it's important to you. Your local Slimming World class offers a very special brand of support and we'd be delighted to welcome you there.

MAXIMISE YOUR HEALTHY EATING

- Eat at least five portions of fresh fruit and vegetables every day. Frozen and canned vegetables can also be used.

- Trim any visible fat off meat and remove any skin from poultry.

- Vary your choices as much as possible to ensure the widest range of nutrients.

- Eat at least two portions of fish a week, of which one should be oily fish.

- Try to avoid eating more than ten eggs per week as these are particularly high in cholesterol. People with high blood cholesterol are advised not to eat more than four eggs per week, although each individual should check with their doctor.

- Aim to keep your salt intake to no more than 6 g a day (about 1 level teaspoon). As well as limiting the amount of table salt you add to food, watch out for salt added to manufactured foods and sauces. Try flavouring foods with herbs and spices instead.

- Remember the latest recommendations regarding intake of fluids, which is to aim for 6-8 cups, mugs or glasses of any type of fluid per day (excluding alcohol).

- Choose a milk allowance each day from the following: 350 ml (12 fl oz) skimmed milk or 250 ml (8 fl oz) semi-skimmed milk or 175 ml (6 fl oz) whole milk or 250 ml (8 fl oz) calcium-enriched soya milk, sweetened or unsweetened.

- Or if you prefer cheese rather than milk, choose a cheese allowance from the following: 25 g (1 oz) Cheddar or 25 g (1 oz) Edam or 25 g (1 oz) Gouda or 40 g (1½ oz) Mozzarella or 40 g (1½ oz) reduced-fat Cheddar/Cheshire.

- Drink black tea, coffee (sweetened with artificial sweetener) and low-calorie drinks freely and use fat-free French or vinaigrette-style salad dressings freely.

- Learn to recognise false appetite. Ask yourself do I really want to eat or am I hungry because someone else is eating/I am bored/I eat when the television is on.

- Give yourself a chance to recognise the signs of being really full – take time to eat, chew thoroughly.

- If you're not sure how hungry you are, and you have eaten a meal recently, do something else for 10 minutes then check your appetite – if it's still there, eat.

- Be aware of what foods you personally enjoy that fill you quickly and what foods keep you full for longest. Make a list of your favourites and keep that list growing.

- Eat whole fruits rather than drinking fruit juices as your daily choice of fruit.

- Top carbohydrate fillers are beans, lentils, wholemeal pasta and spaghetti and brown rice. Potatoes boiled in their skins are better than mashed.

- Vary the sorts of fibre you choose for maximum health benefits. Eat wholemeal varieties of bread and breakfast on a wholegrain cereal.

- If you've been eating a fibre-poor diet, increase fibre-rich foods slowly. Drink plenty of water when increasing fibre intake.

RECIPE SIN VALUES

If you are a member of Slimming World, you will be familiar with the 'Original Day' and 'Green Day' eating plans and the Sin values of foods. The sins listed below for each of the recipes in this book are per portion; the Food Optimising system recommends using between 5 and 20 sins per day.

If you are not a member of Slimming World and would like details of the nearest class to you, telephone the Class Finder service on 01773 521111 between 8am and 8pm from Monday to Friday.

Starters	*Page number*	*Original Day*	*Green Day*
Chicken tikka	30	free	7½
Classic leek and potato soup	20	6	free
Greek-style mushrooms	16	1	1
Hearty bean and vegetable soup	22	11	free
Italian-style bacon soup with pesto	25	1	3
Mexican avocado dip	14	2	2
Peperonata filo tarts	19	3	3
Prawn and melon cocktail	26	2	9½
Smoked fish pâté	28	2	14½

Main Courses			
Cod in parsley sauce	48	1	8½
Garlic chicken and vegetable pot roast	34	free	10½
Greek-style lamb steaks	38	free	11½
Mustard pork steaks with red cabbage	42	2	9
Pan-cooked prawns with garlic and vermouth			
	51	1½	4½
Pork and herb meatballs with ratatouille sauce			
	44	free	7

STARTERS

MEXICAN AVOCADO DIP

SERVES: 4   PREPARATION: 15 MINS

INGREDIENTS

1 large beefsteak tomato
4 spring onions
1 small ripe avocado
2 tbsp lemon juice
115 g (4 oz) low-fat soft cheese
2 tbsp freshly chopped coriander
salt and freshly ground black pepper
a few drops of Tabasco sauce

NUTRITION

Each portion contains:

Energy: 80 calories

Fat: 5 g of which saturates 1 g

1 Remove the stalk from the tomato and finely chop the flesh. Place in a bowl. Trim and finely chop the white and green parts of the spring onions and mix into the tomatoes.

2 Halve the avocado and discard the stone. Peel off the skin from both halves and mash the flesh with the lemon juice. Mix the flesh with the soft cheese.

3 Combine the avocado mixture with the chopped tomato and spring onion along with the coriander, plenty of seasoning and a few drops of Tabasco.

4 Serve with plenty of crisp vegetables like peppers, celery, radishes and cucumber to dip.

COOK'S TIP

This is a lighter version of guacamole, which is usually laden with fat. The dip is full of flavour and is very colourful when served with different raw vegetables to dip into it. It is perfect to serve at parties or as a topping for baked potatoes. Remember, Tabasco sauce is made from spicy red chillies and a few drops will add quite a lot of heat to any dish.

GREEK-STYLE MUSHROOMS

SERVES: 4   PREPARATION: 10 MINS, PLUS COOLING AND CHILLING

COOKING: 5 MINS

INGREDIENTS

225 g (8 oz) baby button mushrooms

225 g (8 oz) open cup mushrooms

285 ml (½ pint) vegetable stock

2 bay leaves

400 g (14 oz) can chopped tomatoes
     with garlic

4 tbsp dry white wine

salt and freshly ground black pepper

4 tbsp freshly chopped parsley

25 g (1 oz) pitted black olives in
     brine, drained and roughly
     chopped

NUTRITION

Each portion contains:

Energy: 50 calories

Fat: 1.5 g of which saturates 0.2 g

1 Wipe the mushrooms. Place the baby button mushrooms in a saucepan. Thickly slice the open cup mushrooms and add to the saucepan along with the stock and bay leaves. Bring to the boil, cover and simmer for 5 minutes until the mushrooms are just tender. Remove from the heat and allow to cool.

2 Drain the mushrooms and discard the bay leaves. Carefully mix in the tomatoes, wine and seasoning. Cover and chill for at least an hour.

3 To serve, sprinkle each portion with chopped parsley and a few chopped olives.

COOK'S TIP

A simple, yet tasty starter making the most of the meaty texture of mushrooms. Experiment with different varieties of mushrooms and serve simply with a few salad leaves. Cans of chopped tomatoes flavoured with garlic are available in most supermarkets.

PEPERONATA FILO TARTS

SERVES: 4   PREPARATION: 15 MINS   COOKING: 50 MINS

INGREDIENTS

1 small red pepper

1 small red onion

1 large beefsteak tomato

salt and freshly ground black pepper

low-fat spray oil

2 x 25 g (1 oz) large sheets frozen
    filo pastry, thawed

1 medium egg, beaten

4 tbsp very low-fat fromage frais

2 level tbsp freshly grated Parmesan
    cheese

1 tsp dried oregano

NUTRITION

Each portion contains:

Energy: 135 calories

Fat: 5 g of which saturates 2 g

1 Preheat the oven to 200°C/400°F/Gas 6. Halve and de-seed the pepper and cut in half again. Peel the onion and cut into quarters. Remove the stalk from the tomato and cut in half.

2 Arrange the vegetables on a non-stick baking sheet or in a small shallow roasting tin. Season well and spray lightly with the oil. Bake in the oven for 25–30 minutes or until tender. Leave the oven on for cooking the pastry tarts.

3 Meanwhile, lay the sheets of pastry on top of each other and cut into six equal pieces, making a total of 12 pieces.

4 Lay one piece of pastry in the base of four 10 cm (4 in) circular non-stick Yorkshire pudding tins. Brush with a little egg and lay another piece on top at a different angle. Brush again and top with the remaining pastry. Each tart is made of three pastry layers. Push in the edges slightly to create a case.

5 Mix the remaining egg with the fromage frais, Parmesan cheese and seasoning.

6 Once the vegetables are cooked, chop them roughly and mix together. Pile into the cases and top with the cheese mixture. Sprinkle with oregano and bake for 15–20 minutes until golden and set. Serve at once.

COOK'S TIP

Wafer-thin layers of pastry are combined with a tasty filling of peppers and onion and topped with a cheesy layer, which sets on baking.

CLASSIC LEEK AND POTATO SOUP

SERVES: 4   PREPARATION: 10 MINS   COOKING: 35 MINS

INGREDIENTS

1 large onion

2 bay leaves

1.2 litres (2 pints) chicken stock

680g (1½ lb) potatoes

1 large leek

salt and freshly ground black pepper

140 g (5 oz) very low-fat fromage
   frais

2 tbsp freshly chopped chives

NUTRITION

Each portion contains:

Energy: 170 calories

Fat: 0.6 g of which saturates 0.1 g

1 Peel and finely chop the onion. Place in a large saucepan along with the bay leaves and 142 ml (¼ pint) of the stock. Bring to the boil, cover and simmer for 5 minutes.

2 Meanwhile, peel and finely dice the potatoes. Trim the leek and slice lengthwise. Rinse under cold water to remove any trapped earth. Shake well to remove excess water and then shred.

3 Add the potato and all but a few shreds of the leek to the saucepan. Pour in the remaining stock and season well. Bring to the boil, cover and simmer for 25 minutes or until tender.

4 Discard the bay leaves, let the mixture cool slightly, then transfer to a food processor or blender. Blend until smooth and return to the saucepan.

5 Stir in the fromage frais and reheat gently without boiling. Adjust the seasoning if necessary. Ladle into warmed soup bowls, sprinkle with black pepper, reserved shredded leek and chopped chives.

COOK'S TIP

Traditionally, this soup has butter and thick cream added to it, but our version is much lighter and allows the subtle flavour of the vegetables to come through. This is the perfect choice for those who prefer a less strongly flavoured soup.

HEARTY BEAN AND VEGETABLE SOUP

SERVES: 4   PREPARATION: 10 MINS   COOKING: 30 MINS

INGREDIENTS

1 medium onion

1 clove garlic

1 tsp dried oregano

285 ml (½ pint) vegetable stock

1 large green pepper

425 g (15 oz) can mixed pulses,
    drained and rinsed

570 ml (1 pint) passata

1 large courgette

315 g (11 oz) can sweetcorn kernels
    in water, drained

salt and freshly ground black pepper

fresh oregano leaves

NUTRITION

Each portion contains:

Energy: 150 calories

Fat: 1 g of which saturates 0.2 g

1 Peel and finely chop the onion and garlic. Place them in a large saucepan along with the oregano and half the stock. Bring to the boil, cover and simmer for 5 minutes.

2 Meanwhile, halve and de-seed the pepper. Cut into small chunks. Stir the pepper, pulses and passata into the onion along with the remaining stock. Bring to the boil, cover and simmer for 10 minutes.

3 Trim and dice the courgette into small chunks and stir into the soup along with the sweetcorn. Simmer for a further 10 minutes. Taste and season.

4 Ladle into warmed soup bowls, garnish with a few fresh oregano leaves and serve.

COOK'S TIP

Using canned pulses and beans saves time and effort. Keep them in the cupboard as a good standby for when you want to make a substantial vegetable stew or soup. They're an excellent source of dietary fibre as well. Passata is a thick tomato sauce available from supermarkets, usually sold in jars.

ITALIAN-STYLE BACON SOUP WITH PESTO

SERVES: 4   PREPARATION: 15 MINS   COOKING: 25 MINS

INGREDIENTS

115 g (4 oz) lean unsmoked rindless
   back bacon

1 large onion

1 large carrot

2 sticks celery

285 ml (½ pint) vegetable stock

1 medium red pepper

1 tsp dried oregano

2 x 400 g (14 oz) can chopped
   tomatoes with garlic

salt and freshly ground black pepper

For the pesto:

4 tbsp very low-fat fromage frais

2 level tbsp freshly grated Parmesan
   cheese

1 clove garlic (optional)

small bunch fresh basil

small basil leaves to garnish

NUTRITION

Each portion contains:

Energy: 143 calories

Fat: 5 g of which saturates 2.5 g

1 Remove and discard any excess fat from the bacon and then finely chop the meat. Place in a large non-stick saucepan. Peel and finely chop the onion and add to the saucepan. Heat gently until the bacon juices run, and then stir fry for 2–3 minutes.

2 Peel and finely chop the carrot. Trim and chop the celery. Stir into the bacon and pour in half the stock. Bring to the boil, cover and simmer for 5 minutes.

3 Halve and de-seed the pepper, then cut into small pieces. Add to the saucepan along with the oregano, tomatoes, remaining stock and seasoning. Bring to the boil, and simmer, uncovered, for 15 minutes until the soup is thick and tender.

4 Meanwhile, prepare the pesto. Mix the fromage frais and Parmesan cheese together. Peel and crush the garlic, if using, and stir into the mixture along with some seasoning. Chop the basil finely and add to the mixture. Cover and chill until required.

5 To serve, ladle the soup into warmed soup bowls. Top each with a spoonful of pesto, sprinkle over black pepper and a few basil leaves.

COOK'S TIP

Pesto sauce is usually high in fat, but this version although lighter, still has all the flavour and is delicious spooned onto a hot, chunky soup such as this. As the pesto melts, it runs into the soup and adds a more intense flavour. Cans of tomatoes flavoured with garlic are widely available in supermarkets.

PRAWN AND MELON COCKTAIL

SERVES: 4   PREPARATION AND COOKING: 25 MINS

INGREDIENTS

8 thin slices lean Parma ham

1 head of radicchio lettuce

½ orange-fleshed melon such as
    charantais

½ green-fleshed melon such as galia

340 g (12 oz) peeled prawns, thawed
    if frozen

For the dressing:

1 level tbsp low-calorie mayonnaise

1 tbsp very low-fat fromage frais

½ tsp mild curry powder

2 level tsp spicy mango chutney

salt and freshly ground black pepper

2 tbsp freshly chopped coriander

NUTRITION

Each portion contains:

Energy: 160 calories

Fat: 3 g of which saturates 0.5 g

1 Preheat the grill to a hot setting. Trim away any excess fat from the ham and lay the slices side by side on the grill rack. Cook under the grill for about a minute, turning, until wrinkled and crispy. Drain and set aside.

2 Trim away the outside leaves from the lettuce. Wash and shake dry, then break up the leaves and arrange on four serving plates.

3 Scoop out the seeds from the melon halves. Trim away the skin and cut the melons into bite-sized pieces. Place them on top of the lettuce. Top with the prawns.

4 To make the dressing, mix together the mayonnaise, fromage frais, curry powder, chutney and seasoning. Spoon on top of the prawns. Arrange the ham on top either whole or broken into pieces. Sprinkle with chopped coriander and serve at once.

COOK'S TIP

This is a variation of the classic starter of the Sixties and Seventies. Here it has been brought right up to date and looks stunning, as well as being remarkably low in fat.

SMOKED FISH PÂTÉ

SERVES: 4   PREPARATION: 20 MINS, PLUS CHILLING

INGREDIENTS

400 g (14 oz) red or pink salmon
  canned in brine, drained
115 g (4 oz) smoked mackerel fillet
115 g (4 oz) quark skimmed milk soft
  cheese
juice of 1 small lemon
salt and freshly ground black pepper
55 g (2 oz) smoked salmon
2 tbsp freshly chopped parsley

NUTRITION

Each portion contains:

Energy: 295 calories

Fat: 16 g of which saturates 3 g

1 Flake the salmon away from the skin and bones and place in a mixing bowl. Skin and flake the mackerel and mix into the salmon.

2 Mix the soft cheese and lemon juice into the fishes until well combined. Taste and season if necessary.

3 Shred or finely chop the smoked salmon and mix into the pâté. If you want a smoother pâté, then blend in a food processor for a few seconds. Cover and chill for 30 minutes.

4 Serve scooped onto serving plates, sprinkled with chopped parsley. Accompany with wedges of lemon to squeeze over, and mixed salad or sticks of raw vegetables.

COOK'S TIP

Very easy to prepare, this pâté also makes a good filling for sandwiches. It can easily be packed in a box for a picnic or packed lunch as it is quite firm once chilled. If you haven't got a food processor, then mash the fish with a fork for a chunkier result.

CHICKEN TIKKA

SERVES: 4   PREPARATION AND COOKING: 30 MINS, PLUS CHILLING

INGREDIENTS

4 x 140 g (5 oz) boneless, skinless
    chicken breasts
salt and freshly ground black pepper
6 tbsp very low-fat natural yogurt
1 level tbsp tomato purée
1 tbsp medium curry powder
1 tbsp lemon juice
2 tbsp freshly chopped coriander

NUTRITION

Each portion contains:

Energy: 200 calories

Fat: 7 g of which saturates 2 g

1 Wash and pat dry the chicken breasts. Using a small sharp knife, slice the breasts three or four times diagonally without cutting right the way through. Season both sides with salt and freshly ground black pepper and place in a shallow dish.

2 Mix the remaining ingredients together and spoon over the chicken, making sure the chicken is completely covered. Cover and chill for at least 30 minutes.

3 Preheat the grill to medium-hot. Line the grill tray with foil and arrange the chicken breasts on the tray. Cook the chicken for 8–10 minutes on each side or until tender and cooked through.

4 Drain the chicken and serve with raita (diced cucumber and yogurt) and a tomato, onion and mixed green leaf salad.

COOK'S TIP

Chicken tikka is now one of Britain's favourite meals, and there's no reason at all why slimmers should miss out on it! This quick and easy version tastes fantastic and is ideal served as a starter. The longer you let the chicken marinate in the spicy yogurt, the better the flavour. But if time is short, the 30 minutes estimated here is fine.

MAIN
courses

GARLIC CHICKEN AND VEGETABLE POT ROAST

SERVES: 4   PREPARATION: 15 MINS   COOKING: 1 HOUR 30 MINS

INGREDIENTS

2 small red peppers

2 small green peppers

225 g (8 oz) shallots or small
onions

1 bulb fennel

1.4 kg (3 lb) oven-ready chicken

salt and freshly ground black pepper

1 small lemon

145 ml (¼ pint) chicken stock

2 sprigs each of fresh thyme,
rosemary and tarragon, plus
extra to garnish

2 bay leaves

1 bulb garlic

1 tbsp fennel seeds

NUTRITION

Each portion contains:

Energy: 240 calories

Fat: 7 g of which saturates 2 g

1 Preheat the oven to 180°C/350°F/Gas 4. Halve and de-seed the peppers and cut into wide slices. Place in the bottom of a large oval casserole with a tight-fitting lid. Peel and halve the shallots or onions and mix into the peppers. Trim the fennel and slice thickly. Place in the casserole.

2 Wash and pat dry the chicken and season inside and out. Halve the lemon and place inside the chicken. Place the chicken on top of the vegetables and pull some of the vegetables up around the sides of the chicken. Pour in the stock.

3 Tie the herbs together and place in the casserole. Break the bulb of garlic up and peel away the outer paper but do not peel the cloves. Scatter the cloves over the chicken and vegetables, and sprinkle with the fennel seeds.

4 Cover the casserole with a sheet of foil and then place the lid on top. Bake for 1¼–1½ hours until tender and cooked through and the juices run clear when a skewer is inserted into the breast and legs.

5 Drain the chicken and vegetables and place on a warmed serving platter. Discard the lemon halves. Remove the skin from the chicken and peel the cloves of garlic before eating. Garnish with a few fresh herbs and serve with the vegetables.

THAI GREEN CHICKEN CURRY

SERVES: 4   PREPARATION AND COOKING: 30 MINS

INGREDIENTS

450 g (1 lb) boneless, skinless
    chicken pieces
2 cloves garlic
2 shallots
2.5 cm (1 in) piece root ginger
1 green chilli
1 tsp coriander seeds
1 tsp salt
1 lime
2 x 15 g (½ oz) packs fresh
    coriander
2 level tsp cornflour
25 g (1 oz) block creamed coconut

For the relish:
115 g (4 oz) fresh pineapple
1 small green pepper
1 small red chilli (optional)

coriander sprig to garnish

NUTRITION

Each portion contains:

Energy: 215 calories

Fat: 10 g of which saturates 6 g

1 Cut the chicken into 2.5 cm (1 in) cubes and place in a bowl.

2 Peel the garlic, shallots and ginger. Halve and de-seed the chilli and lightly crush the coriander seeds. Place all these ingredients in a food processor or blender and add the salt.

3 Finely grate the lime rind, extract the juice and add these to the garlic mixture along with one pack of fresh coriander. Process to form a smooth paste and then stir into the chicken along with the cornflour. Mix well.

4 Grate the coconut into a shallow pan and pour over 284 ml (½ pint) water. Bring to the boil, stirring until dissolved. Add the chicken and mix well. Bring back to the boil, cover and simmer for 15 minutes or until the chicken is cooked through.

5 Meanwhile, to make the relish, finely chop the pineapple and place in a small bowl. Halve, de-seed and finely chop the pepper and chilli, if using, and finely chop the remaining pack of fresh coriander. Mix the pepper, chilli and coriander into the pineapple and chill in the fridge until required.

6 Serve the chicken garnished with fresh coriander, accompanied with the pineapple relish and green vegetables.

COOK'S TIP

Here is brilliant idea for a low-fat speedy supper with a hint of spice. From start to finish this tasty dish will take you only 30 minutes to prepare.

GREEK-STYLE LAMB STEAKS

SERVES: 4   PREPARATION: 10 MINS   COOKING: 1 HOUR 30 MINS

INGREDIENTS

2 medium red onions

2 cloves garlic

2 tbsp lemon juice

4 medium tomatoes

few sprigs fresh rosemary

4 x 145 g (5 oz) lean lamb steaks

salt and freshly ground black pepper

fresh rosemary to garnish

NUTRITION

Each portion contains:

Energy: 280 calories

Fat: 13 g of which saturates 6 g

1 Preheat the oven to 180°C/350°F/Gas 4. Peel the onions and garlic. Slice the onions into thin wedges and toss in the lemon juice. Thinly slice the garlic. Remove the stalks from the tomatoes and cut into quarters.

2 Arrange the onions, garlic and tomatoes in the base of a casserole dish with a tight-fitting lid and sprinkle with rosemary sprigs.

3 Trim away any excess fat from the lamb steaks and season on both sides. Arrange on top of the vegetables. Cover with a layer of foil and then the lid. Bake in the oven for about 1½ hours or until very tender.

4 Drain and serve garnished with fresh rosemary, and accompanied with green vegetables or a crisp Greek-style salad.

COOK'S TIP

This is inspired by the traditional Greek dish *kleftico*. This is usually made using a joint of lamb which is slowly cooked in a clay oven. But it works just as well using lamb steaks, and with this method they come out of the oven beautifully tender and moist.

REDCURRANT LAMB WITH LEEK AND SWEDE MASH

SERVES: 4   PREPARATION AND COOKING: 30 MINS

INGREDIENTS
For the mash:
450 g (1 lb) swede
450 g (1 lb) leeks
145 ml (¼ pint) vegetable stock
1 tbsp very low-fat fromage frais

4 x 100 g (3½ oz) lean boneless
    lamb leg steaks
4 level tbsp redcurrant jelly
1 tsp dried rosemary
garlic salt and freshly ground black
    pepper

NUTRITION
Each portion contains:
Energy: 260 calories
Fat: 10 g of which saturates 4 g

1   Peel the swede and cut into small cubes. Place in a saucepan and cover with water. Bring to the boil and cook for 8-10 minutes until softened. Drain well.

2   Trim the leeks and rinse under running water. Slice and place in a saucepan with the stock. Bring to the boil, cover and simmer for 5 minutes until tender. Drain, reserving the cooking liquid.

3   Place the swede and leeks in a bowl and mash with a potato masher. Season and mix in the fromage frais. Set aside and keep warm.

4   Preheat the grill to a medium-hot setting. Trim lamb if necessary and arrange on the grill rack. Melt 2 tbsp of the redcurrant jelly in a small saucepan and add the rosemary and seasoning. Brush the redcurrant mixture over the lamb and grill for 7 minutes. Turn, brush again and cook for a further 7–8 minutes or until cooked to your liking.

5   In a saucepan, melt the remaining redcurrant jelly and blend in the reserved leek cooking liquid. Bring to the boil and boil rapidly for 2 minutes until the sauce has thickened slightly.

7   To serve, pile some swede and leek mash onto a warmed serving plate, top with a lamb steak and spoon over a little redcurrant jelly sauce. Serve with a selection of steamed vegetables.

MUSTARD PORK STEAKS WITH RED CABBAGE

SERVES: 4   PREPARATION AND COOKING: 30 MINS

INGREDIENTS

½ medium red cabbage

2 red onions

25 g (1 oz) low-fat spread

145 ml (¼ pint) red wine vinegar

1 tsp ground cinnamon

salt and freshly ground black pepper

1–2 tbsp granular artificial
    sweetener

4 x 115 g (4 oz) lean boneless pork
    steaks

2 level tbsp wholegrain mustard

NUTRITION

Each portion contains:

Energy: 230 calories

Fat: 11 g of which saturates 4 g

1 Trim the cabbage and finely shred. Peel and finely chop the onions.

2 In a large saucepan, melt the low-fat spread over a low heat. Stir in the cabbage and onion and mix well to coat. Add the vinegar, cinnamon, seasoning and 4 tbsp water. Bring to the boil, cover and simmer for 15 minutes. Stir in the artificial sweetener to taste.

3 Meanwhile, trim the pork if necessary. Season to taste and spread mustard onto both sides.

4 Preheat the grill to a medium-hot setting. Arrange the pork steaks on the grill rack and cook for 7 minutes. Turn over and grill for a further 7–8 minutes or until cooked through.

5 To serve, drain the cabbage and pile onto a warmed serving plate. Top with a pork steak and serve immediately.

COOK'S TIP

This dish is perfect for winter days accompanied by broccoli, carrots and mashed swede. It is equally delicious served with a generous salad.

PORK AND HERB MEATBALLS WITH RATATOUILLE SAUCE

SERVES: 4   PREPARATION: 20 MINS, PLUS CHILLING

COOKING: 20 MINS

INGREDIENTS

For the meatballs:

4 spring onions

450 g (1 lb) extra lean minced pork

1 tsp dried mixed herbs

salt and freshly ground black pepper

For the sauce:

1 small onion

1 small yellow pepper

1 small courgette

1 baby aubergine

1 bay leaf

400 g (14 oz) can chopped
     tomatoes with garlic

2 tbsp freshly chopped parsley

NUTRITION

Each portion contains:

Energy: 210 calories

Fat: 8 g of which saturates 3 g

1 To make the meatballs, trim and finely chop the white and green parts of the spring onions. Place in a mixing bowl and add the minced pork, dried herbs and plenty of seasoning. Mix well to combine and then divide into twenty portions. Form into small balls and place on a plate lined with baking parchment. Cover and chill for 30 minutes.

2 Meanwhile prepare the sauce. Peel the onion and chop finely. Halve and de-seed the pepper and chop finely. Trim the courgette and aubergine and chop finely. Place in a saucepan along with the bay leaf and chopped tomatoes. Season well, bring to the boil and simmer for 10 minutes until tender. Set aside until ready to serve.

3 Preheat the grill to a medium-hot setting. Arrange the meatballs on the grill rack and cook for 8–10 minutes, turning frequently or until golden and cooked through. Drain well.

4 Reheat the sauce until piping hot, discard the bay leaf and serve the meatballs with the sauce, sprinkled with chopped parsley.

COOK'S TIP

Tender morsels of herby lean pork are grilled and served on a bed of colourful Mediterranean vegetables. Use minced beef, lamb or chicken as an alternative if preferred. Tinned chopped tomatoes flavoured with garlic are widely available.

STEAK AND MUSHROOM PIE

SERVES: 4   PREPARATION: 15 MINS, PLUS COOLING

COOKING: 2 HOURS 10 MINS

INGREDIENTS

1 medium onion

680 g (1½ lb) lean cubed braising
    steak

1 level tbsp cornflour

2 bay leaves

salt and freshly ground black pepper

285 ml (½ pint) beef stock

225 g (8 oz) closed cup mushrooms

3 x 25 g (1 oz) sheets filo pastry

1 medium egg, beaten

NUTRITION

Each portion contains:

Energy: 335 calories

Fat: 10 g of which saturates 4 g

1 Peel and slice the onion and place in a pan. Remove all visible fat from the steak, toss in the cornflour and add it to the pan with the bay leaves and seasoning. Add the stock and about 142 ml (¼ pint) water to just cover the beef. Bring to the boil, cover and simmer for 1½ hours until the beef is tender. Cool, then discard the bay leaves.

2 Preheat the oven to 220°C/425°F/Gas 7. Quarter the mushrooms and place in a 1140 ml (2 pint) pie dish. Add the beef and onions using a slotted spoon, and pour over about 200 ml (7 fl oz) of the cooking liquid to come halfway up the dish. The meat will rise to the top, but as the mushrooms cook down, the level within the dish will sink.

3. Brush each sheet of pastry with egg, lightly scrunch up and place on top of the meat, pulling the sheets out to make sure all the meat is covered. Brush generously with egg and bake for 20 minutes. Lower the heat to 180°C/350°F/Gas 4 and continue to cook for a further 20 minutes until golden and hot. Serve with green vegetables.

COOK'S TIP

Don't be put off by the long cooking time on this recipe – the actual preparation time is quick. We guarantee that the rich flavour and crisp pastry make it well worth the wait!

COD IN PARSLEY SAUCE

SERVES: 4   PREPARATION AND COOKING: 20 MINS

INGREDIENTS

4 x 170 g (6 oz) skinless thick cod
   fillets
grated rind and juice of 1 small
   lemon
salt and freshly ground black pepper
8 bay leaves

For the sauce:
2 level tsp cornflour
145 ml (¼ pint) skimmed milk
145 ml (¼ pint) fish or vegetable
   stock
115 g (4 oz) very low-fat fromage
   frais
4 tbsp freshly chopped parsley

NUTRITION

Each portion contains:

Energy: 180 calories

Fat: 1.5 g of which saturates 0.2 g

1 Bring a large saucepan of water to the boil. Place the fish over the water in a steaming compartment, colander or large sieve. Sprinkle with the lemon rind, juice and black pepper. Add the bay leaves, cover and steam for 7–8 minutes or until cooked through.

2 Meanwhile, blend the cornflour with a little of the milk to form a paste. Pour into a saucepan with the rest of the milk and the stock. Bring to the boil, stirring, and cook gently for 1 minute until thickened.

3 Remove from the heat and cool for 5 minutes. Stir in the fromage frais and parsley. Season to taste and return to the heat. Heat through over a low heat until hot – do not allow to boil.

4 Drain the fish and discard the bay leaves. Place on warmed plates and spoon over the sauce. Accompany with fresh vegetables.

COOK'S TIP
An old family favourite has been given a makeover here, reducing the fat levels but still tantalising your tastebuds.

PAN-COOKED PRAWNS WITH GARLIC AND VERMOUTH

SERVES: 4   PREPARATION AND COOKING: 10 MINS

INGREDIENTS

4 cloves garlic

24 large raw prawns in their shells

2 tsp olive oil

juice of 1 lemon

2 tbsp dry white vermouth

salt and freshly ground black pepper

2 tbsp freshly chopped parsley

NUTRITION

Each portion contains:

Energy: 60 calories

Fat: 2 g of which saturates 0.5 g

1 Peel and slice the garlic. Wash the prawns and pat dry with absorbent kitchen paper.

2 Heat the oil in a wok or large frying pan until hot and add the garlic then the prawns in a single layer – cook the prawns in two batches if necessary – turning frequently. Stir-fry for 2 minutes until the prawns are coated with the oil. Add the lemon juice and simmer, stirring, for a further 2 minutes until all the prawns are pink.

3 Sprinkle with vermouth and season to taste. Sprinkle with parsley and serve immediately.

COOK'S TIP

Quite an unusual way to cook prawns, this dish makes a delicious starter or main course. As it only takes 10 minutes to prepare it's an ideal dish to serve when entertaining or if you are in a hurry. Large prawns like these are expensive but they have a delicious taste and make a stunning course for a special dinner. You can use raw unpeeled tiger prawns as a less expensive alternative, and you will need to allow about 8–10 per person. White wine can be used instead of vermouth, if you wish.

VEGETABLE LASAGNE

SERVES: 4   PREPARATION AND COOKING: 1 HOUR

INGREDIENTS

For the vegetable sauce:

2 medium red onions

1 clove garlic

1 medium red pepper

1 medium yellow pepper

1 medium aubergine

1 medium courgettes

2 x 400 g (14 oz) cans chopped
  tomatoes with herbs

salt and freshly ground black pepper

2 level tbsp tomato purée

For the white sauce:

2 level tbsp cornflour

285 ml (½ pint) skimmed milk

145 ml (¼ pint) very low-fat
  fromage frais

6 no-pre-cook lasagne sheets

4 level tbsp freshly grated Parmesan
  cheese

NUTRITION

Each portion contains:

Energy: 290 calories

Fat: 6 g of which saturates 3 g

1 Preheat the oven to 200°C/400°F/Gas 6. For the vegetable sauce, peel and finely chop the onions and garlic. Wash and de-seed the peppers. Dice the red pepper and cut the yellow pepper into thin strips. Wash and trim the aubergine and courgettes. Dice the aubergine and thinly slice the courgettes.

2 Place the onion, garlic and peppers in a large pan, stir in the canned tomatoes and season. Mix well, bring to the boil, cover and simmer for 10 minutes, stirring after 5 minutes. Add the aubergine and courgettes and cook, uncovered, for 10 minutes, stirring occasionally. Stir in the tomato purée.

3 Meanwhile, make the white sauce. Blend the cornflour with a little of the milk. Pour the remaining milk into a pan, bring to the boil, then add the cornflour mixture and cook for 1–2 minutes until thick, stirring constantly. Remove from the heat and gradually beat in the fromage frais. Season well.

4 Spoon half the vegetable sauce into an ovenproof baking dish. Lay three lasagne sheets on top, and cover with the remaining vegetable sauce. Top with the remaining lasagne and cover with the white sauce. Sprinkle with cheese and bake in the oven for 25–30 minutes until golden and tender.

SPICY BULGUR WHEAT WITH APRICOTS

SERVES: 4   PREPARATION: 12 MINS, PLUS STANDING

COOKING: 12 MINS

INGREDIENTS

1 large red onion

1 tbsp lemon juice

225 g (8 oz) bulgur wheat

850 ml (1½ pints) vegetable stock

115 g (4 oz) no-need-to-soak dried
  apricots

400 g (14 oz) can chickpeas,
  drained and rinsed

1 tsp ground cinnamon

salt and freshly ground black pepper

¼ cucumber

15 g (½ oz) pack fresh coriander

115 g (4 oz) very low-fat natural
  yogurt

NUTRITION

Each portion contains:

Energy: 380 calories

Fat: 4 g of which saturates 0.5 g

1 Peel and finely slice the onion and toss in the lemon juice. Place in a large saucepan along with the bulgur wheat and stock. Bring to the boil, cover and simmer for 10 minutes.

2 Meanwhile, finely slice the apricots. Stir into the bulgur wheat along with the chickpeas, cinnamon and plenty of seasoning. Cover, remove from the heat and leave to stand for 10 minutes until all the stock has been absorbed by the bulgur wheat.

3 Meanwhile, finely chop the cucumber and coriander. Serve the bulgur wheat with the cucumber, coriander and yogurt on the side.

COOK'S TIP

This Middle Eastern-style dish (also known as tabbouleh) is usually laced with olive oil, but this healthier version is so packed with the rich flavours of lemon juice, cinnamon and dried apricots that you really won't miss the oil at all. This dish is delicious served as a salad – simply allow it to cool completely and chill until required.

ROOT VEGETABLE AND LENTIL CASSEROLE

SERVES: 4   PREPARATION: 15 MINS   COOKING: 40 MINS

INGREDIENTS

1 medium onion
2 celery sticks
850 ml (1½ pints) vegetable stock
225 g (8 oz) carrots
225 g (8 oz) potatoes
225 g (8 oz) parsnips
225 g (8 oz) swede
1 large leek
1 tsp paprika
1 tsp ground cumin
1 tsp ground coriander
1 tsp mustard seeds, crushed
salt and freshly ground black pepper
115 g (4 oz) red lentils
2 tbsp freshly chopped coriander

NUTRITION

Each portion contains:

Energy: 225 calories

Fat: 2 g of which saturates 0.3 g

1 Peel the onion and slice thinly. Trim and slice the celery. Place in a large saucepan with 140 ml (¼ pint) stock. Bring to the boil, cover and simmer for 5 minutes.

2 Meanwhile, peel and slice the carrots. Peel the potatoes, parsnips and swede and cut into small chunks. Trim and slice the leek lengthwise and rinse under running water to flush out any trapped earth. Shake well and slice thickly.

3 Stir the vegetables into the saucepan along with the remaining stock, spices, plenty of seasoning and the lentils. Bring to the boil, cover and cook for 30 minutes or until the vegetables are tender.

4 Serve the casserole sprinkled with chopped coriander and accompanied by green vegetables.

COOK'S TIP

This is a hearty, satisfying combination of comforting vegetables cooked in a mildly spicy stock, thickened with red lentils. Once the vegetables have been prepared, the casserole can be left to cook on its own.

SWEETCORN AND PASTA BAKE

SERVES 4   PREPARATION AND COOKING: 1 HOUR

INGREDIENTS

225 g (8 oz) small dried pasta
    shapes
1 bunch spring onions
1 small red pepper
225 g (8 oz) canned sweetcorn
    kernels, drained
200 g (7 oz) low-fat soft cheese
400 g (14 oz) very low-fat fromage
    frais
2 large eggs, beaten
salt and freshly ground black pepper
fresh chives

NUTRITION

Each portion contains:

Energy: 430 calories

Fat: 9 g of which saturates 4 g

1 Preheat the oven to 200°C/400°F/Gas 6. Bring a large saucepan of lightly salted water to the boil and cook the pasta until it is just tender. Drain well.

2 Meanwhile, trim and chop the spring onions and halve, de-seed and chop the pepper. Place in a heatproof mixing bowl and stir in the sweetcorn, soft cheese, fromage frais and eggs. Beat until well blended.

3 Mix in the drained pasta and add plenty of seasoning. Pile into an ovenproof dish and level the surface. Stand the dish in a roasting tin and pour in sufficient boiling water to come half way up the side of the dish. Bake in the oven for 30–35 minutes until firm and golden.

4 Sprinkle with fresh chives and serve with a crisp salad.

COOK'S TIP

The ultimate comfort food, this pasta bake has a delicious creamy sauce. Small pasta shapes work best in this recipe, but you could use short lengths of spaghetti or tagliatelle as an alternative. Do not over-cook the pasta in step 1 as it will continue to soften when in the oven.

ROAST BEEF WITH MEXICAN-STYLE COLESLAW

SERVES: 4 PREPARATION: 20 MINS, PLUS CHILLING

INGREDIENTS

½ red cabbage

1 small onion

1 small red pepper

115 g (4 oz) radishes

2 tbsp freshly chopped coriander

4 tbsp very low-fat fromage frais

2 level tsp chilli sauce

1 lime

salt and freshly ground black pepper

340 g (12 oz) lean roast beef,
   thinly sliced

a few coriander leaves to garnish

NUTRITION

Each portion contains:

Energy: 235 calories

Fat: 11 g of which saturates 4.5 g

1 Remove the central stalk from the cabbage and finely shred the leaves. Peel and finely chop the onion. Wash and dry the pepper, then cut in half, de-seed and finely chop. Wash, dry and grate the radishes. Place all the vegetables in a bowl and mix in the chopped coriander.

2 Mix the fromage frais with the chilli sauce. Finely grate the rind from the lime, taking care not to use the bitter white pith, and extract the juice. Mix these into the fromage frais and season well.

3 Stir the chilli dressing into the vegetables and mix well. Cover and chill for 30 minutes.

4 Divide the beef between four serving plates and spoon on the coleslaw. Serve sprinkled with fresh coriander.

COOK'S TIP

This is an excellent recipe for using up leftover cooked meat. Alternatively, you can buy ready-sliced cooked beef or other meat from the delicatessen or supermarket. Trim any fat from the meat before serving.

SLIMMING WORLD'S SIN-FREE CHIPS

SERVES: 4   PREPARATION AND COOKING: 40 MINS

INGREDIENTS

910 g (2 lb) medium-sized Maris
    Piper potatoes
low-fat spray oil
crushed sea salt and malt vinegar
    (optional)

NUTRITION

Each portion contains:

Energy: 180 calories

Fat: 1 g of which saturates 0.1 g

1 Preheat oven to 240°C/475°F/Gas 9. Peel the potatoes using a potato peeler and remove any blemishes or 'eyes'. Slice lengthwise into approximately 1 cm (½ in) thick rectangular chips.

2 Bring a large saucepan of salted water to the boil. Add the chips and cook for 4 minutes. Drain and leave aside for 10 minutes to dry.

3 Return the chips to the dry saucepan, cover with a lid and shake to 'rough up' the edges of the chips – this 'roughness' is important to the texture of the chips.

4 Spray a metal baking tray with the oil. Transfer the chips to the tray and spray lightly with the oil. Bake in the oven for 20–25 minutes, turning occasionally, until golden brown on all sides. Drain the chips on absorbent kitchen paper and serve with salt and vinegar.

COOK'S TIP

Chips are high on the list of foods that are hard to give up when you are losing weight – and the good news is that with our low-fat version you don't have to!

SPICY RED ROAST VEGETABLES

SERVES: 4   PREPARATION: 20 MINS   COOKING: 40 MINS

INGREDIENTS

1 medium red pepper

1 medium yellow pepper

8 shallots or baby onions

1 large courgette

1 bulb fennel

115 g (4 oz) baby corn

170 g (6 oz) large chestnut or large
    closed cup mushrooms

1 clove garlic

3 tbsp dark soy sauce

3 tbsp passata

1 tsp Chinese five spice powder

½–1 tsp hot chilli powder

1 level tbsp clear honey

NUTRITION

Each portion contains:

Energy: 85 calories

Fat: 1 g of which saturates 0.2 g

1 Preheat the oven to 220°C/425°F/Gas 7. Halve and de-seed the peppers, and cut each half in half again. Peel the shallots or baby onions. Trim the courgette and cut diagonally into 1 cm (½ in) thick slices. Trim and quarter the fennel lengthwise. Trim the baby corn. Wipe the mushrooms. Peel and crush the garlic.

2 Place the peppers, onions, fennel and garlic in a large bowl. Mix the soy sauce, passata, five spice powder, chilli powder and honey together and toss into the vegetables.

3 Transfer the vegetables to a large shallow non-stick baking sheet using a draining spoon. Bake in the oven for 20 minutes, turning and basting occasionally.

4 Meanwhile, toss the courgette, mushrooms and baby corn in the remaining sauce. Transfer to the baking sheet with the other vegetables once the 20 minutes are up. Cook for a further 15–20 minutes until the vegetables are rich brown and tender. Serve immediately.

COOK'S TIP

This spicy sauce is an excellent way to liven up vegetables. The soy sauce and passata give the vegetables a rich, browny-red colour together with a deliciously savoury flavour. You won't need to season these vegetables as soy sauce is salty enough. Passata is a thick tomato sauce sold by supermarkets, usually in jars.

STIR-FRIED SUMMER VEGETABLES

SERVES: 4   PREPARATION: 15 MINS   COOKING: 10 MINS

INGREDIENTS

85 g (3 oz) sugar snap peas

85 g (3 oz) baby carrots

85 g (3 oz) thin green beans

85 g (3 oz) fine asparagus spears

1 medium leek

low-fat spray oil

2 tbsp unsweetened orange juice

2 tbsp light soy sauce

2 level tsp clear honey

85 g (3 oz) beansprouts

½ tsp finely grated orange rind

1 tbsp freshly chopped chives

NUTRITION

Each portion contains:

Energy: 55 calories

Fat: 1 g of which saturates 0.2 g

1 Trim the sugar snap peas. Scrub and trim the baby carrots. Top the green beans. Cut the woody ends from the asparagus. Trim the leek and slice lengthwise. Rinse under cold running water to remove any trapped earth, then shred finely.

2 Spray a non-stick wok or large frying pan lightly with the oil and heat until hot. Stir-fry the leek for 2 minutes until wilted. Add the carrots, green beans and asparagus along with the orange juice and stir-fry for 3 minutes.

3 Add the sugar snap peas, soy sauce and honey and stir fry for a further 2 minutes. Add the beansprouts and orange rind and stir-fry for a further minute or until the vegetables are cooked to your liking.

4 Serve immediately sprinkled with the chopped chives.

COOK'S TIP

This is an alternative to a traditional Oriental stir-fry, making the most of the delicate flavours of summer vegetables. It is important to keep the vegetables moving in the wok while they are cooking to ensure they all cook evenly.

SALMON AND ASPARAGUS SALAD

SERVES: 4   PREPARATION AND COOKING: 25 MINS, PLUS COOLING AND CHILLING

INGREDIENTS

4 x 170 g (6 oz) salmon fillets

1 bay leaf

285 ml (½ pint) vegetable stock

225 g (8 oz) fine asparagus spears

For the dressing:

4 tbsp very low-fat fromage frais

5 cm (2 in) piece cucumber, finely
    chopped

2 tbsp freshly chopped herbs such
    as parsley, tarragon and dill

½ tsp fine lemon rind

1 tbsp lemon juice

salt and freshly ground black pepper

For the salad:

1 bunch watercress

2 cartons mustard and cress

¼ cucumber

lemon wedges to garnish

NUTRITION

Each portion contains:

Energy: 350 calories

Fat: 21 g of which saturates 4 g

1 Using a sharp knife, cut the skin off the salmon. Wash and pat dry the fillets and place them in a frying pan with the bay leaf. Pour over the stock, bring to the boil, cover and simmer gently for 5–6 minutes or until cooked through. Allow to cool, then drain and chill for 30 minutes.

2 Meanwhile, bring a large saucepan of water to the boil. Trim the woody ends from the asparagus, and then blanch the spears for 2–3 minutes until just tender. Drain and cool under cold running water. Chill until required.

3 Mix all of the dressing ingredients together and chill until required.

4 To serve, wash and trim the watercress and mustard and cress. Wash and thinly slice the cucumber. Line a large serving platter or four individual plates with these salads and then top with the chilled salmon and a few asparagus spears. Garnish with lemon wedges and serve with the herby dressing.

COOK'S TIP

Salmon and asparagus complement one another perfectly. As you can prepare everything ready in advance, this dish makes an ideal quick lunch or supper.

TURKEY AND CRANBERRY SALAD

SERVES: 4   PREPARATION: 20 MINS, PLUS CHILLING

INGREDIENTS

450 g (1 lb) skinless lean cooked
   turkey meat
4 tbsp very low-fat fromage frais
2 level tbsp low-calorie mayonnaise
1 level tbsp cranberry sauce
salt and freshly ground black pepper
1 bunch watercress
2 stalks celery with leaves
2 eating apples
1 tbsp lemon juice
1 large green pepper

NUTRITION

Each portion contains:

Energy: 230 calories

Fat: 4 g of which saturates 0.5 g

1 Cut the turkey into bite-sized pieces and place in a bowl. Mix together the fromage frais, mayonnaise, cranberry sauce and seasoning and mix into the turkey. Cover and chill for 30 minutes.

2 Meanwhile, wash the watercress and shake to remove excess water. Trim and place in a large bowl. Reserving the celery leaves, trim and chop the stalks, and add to the watercress. Core and chop the apples. Toss in the lemon juice. Halve, de-seed and chop the pepper and mix into the watercress along with the apples.

3 When ready to serve, pile the vegetables onto serving plates and top each portion with the creamy turkey mixture. Garnish with the reserved celery leaves.

COOK'S TIP

This Christmassy mixture of turkey and cranberry sauce is an excellent recipe to try at Christmas time when you're wondering how to use up the leftovers. Cooked chicken or ham would also make a good salad.

DESSERTS

MINTY APPLE CHEESECAKE

SERVES: 6 PREPARATION: 20 MINS, PLUS COOLING AND SETTING
COOKING: 10 MINS

INGREDIENTS

450 g (1 lb) cooking apples

juice of 2 lemons

10 sponge fingers

1 sachet powdered gelatine

255 g (9 oz) low-fat soft cheese

255 g (9 oz) very low-fat fromage frais

2 tsp mint sauce

3–4 tbsp granulated artificial sweetener

1 red-skinned eating apple

mint leaves to decorate

NUTRITION

Each portion contains:

Energy: 175 calories

Fat: 1.7 g of which saturates 0.5 g

1 Peel, core and chop the cooking apples. Place in a saucepan with half the lemon juice and 1 tbsp water. Bring to the boil, cover and simmer for 5 minutes until soft and pulpy. Allow to cool.

2 Meanwhile, line a 20 cm (8 in) square tin with layers of cling film so there are no gaps (this will make it easier to remove the finished cheesecake from the tin). Arrange the sponge fingers side by side in the bottom of the tin, trimming them to fit as necessary. Dissolve the gelatine in 4 tbsp boiling water and set aside to cool.

3 In a mixing bowl, beat together the cheese, fromage frais and mint sauce. Stir in the cooled apple and add sweetener to taste. Stir in the gelatine and mix well. Spoon over the sponge fingers, smooth the top and chill for 2 hours until set.

4 Core the eating apple and cut into thin slices. Place in a small saucepan with the remaining lemon juice and gently bring to the boil. Cover and simmer for 2–3 minutes until tender. Allow to cool.

5 To serve, carefully remove the cheesecake from the tin and cut it into six pieces. Top each piece with a few of the apple slices and mint leaves to decorate.

STRAWBERRY SHORTCAKE SUNDAES

SERVES: 4   PREPARATION: 15 MINS

INGREDIENTS

340 g (12 oz) strawberries

285 g (10 oz) very low-fat fromage frais

few drops almond essence

1–2 tbsp granulated artificial sweetener

4 x butter crunch biscuits

4 x 55 g (2 oz) scoops low-fat vanilla ice cream

NUTRITION

Each portion contains:

Energy: 150 calories

Fat: 6 g of which saturates 1 g

1 Reserving four strawberries for decoration, wash and hull the rest, then slice thinly. Place half in a food processor or blender and blend for a few seconds until smooth and puréed.

2 Mix the fromage frais with sufficient almond essence and sweetener to taste.

3 Crush the biscuits finely.

4 To assemble, divide the sliced strawberries between four sundae glasses. Pour the strawberry purée over the strawberries, reserving a little purée for decoration. Sprinkle over the crushed biscuits and then spoon in the fromage frais. Top with ice cream and strawberry halves, drizzle with the reserved purée and serve immediately.

COOK'S TIP

A simple yet very delicious and decadent dessert, it is also equally good made with raspberries.

PIMMS COCKTAIL JELLIES

SERVES: 4 PREPARATION: 20 MINS, PLUS SETTING

INGREDIENTS

1 sachet powdered gelatine

1 large orange

1 eating apple

juice of 1 lemon

100 ml (3½ fl oz) Pimms

425 ml (¾ pint) diet lemonade

mint sprigs to decorate

NUTRITION

Each portion contains:

Energy: 60 calories

Fat: 0 g fat of which saturates 0 g

1 Pour 4 tbsp boiling water over the gelatine and stir until dissolved, then set aside.

2 Slice off the top and bottom from the orange, then slice off the skin taking away as much of the pith as possible. Slice in between each segment to release the flesh and place in a bowl with any juice that runs out.

3 Core and finely chop the apple and toss in the lemon juice to prevent it from turning brown. Mix into the orange segments. Divide between four serving glasses.

4 Mix the Pimms with the gelatine and lemonade and pour over the fruit. Chill in the fridge for 1–2 hours until set. Serve decorated with sprigs of mint.

COOK'S TIP

A jelly for grown-ups! Bring back the flavours of summer with this fruity, set cocktail, and serve with a cucumber garnish for authenticity. If you wish, make the jellies in individual moulds and turn them out onto serving plates.

BLACKBERRY AND APPLE TANSY

SERVES: 4   PREPARATION: 10 MINS   COOKING: 15 MINS

INGREDIENTS

450 g (1 lb) cooking apples

juice of 1 lemon

225 g (8 oz) blackberries, thawed if frozen

4 medium eggs

1 tsp ground cinnamon

4 tbsp skimmed milk

2–3 tbsp granulated artificial sweetener

1 level tbsp icing sugar

NUTRITION

Each portion contains:

Energy: 160 calories

Fat: 7 g of which saturates 2 g

1   Peel, core and cut the apples into thin wedges. Place in a small saucepan and toss in the lemon juice and 1 tbsp water. Bring to the boil, cover and simmer for 3–4 minutes or until the apple wedges are just tender but still holding their shape.

2   Transfer the apples to a medium-sized non-stick frying pan using a draining spoon and arrange them evenly over the bottom of the pan. If using fresh blackberries, wash them, and then sprinkle them over the apples in the pan.

3   Beat the eggs together with the cinnamon, milk and sweetener to taste. Pour over the fruit. Cook over a medium heat for 7–8 minutes or until just set.

4   Preheat the grill to a hot setting. Thickly dust the egg with icing sugar and cook under the grill for 1–2 minutes or until lightly golden and caramelized.

5   Serve hot, cut into wedges, accompanied with a spoonful of very low-fat fromage frais.

COOK'S TIP

A traditional West Country pudding made from eggs, a tansy is really a sweet omelette with fruit set in it. This low-fat version is very light and has a melt-in-the-mouth texture. If blackberries are unavailable, raspberries would make an excellent and colourful alternative.

CHOCOLATE ORANGE MOUSSE

SERVES: 4   PREPARATION: 20 MINS, PLUS COOLING AND CHILLING

INGREDIENTS

1 x 15 g (½ oz) sachet sugar-free
   orange jelly crystals

500 g (1 lb 2 oz) very low-fat
   fromage frais

25 g (1 oz) cocoa powder

2 large egg whites

1–2 tbsp granulated artificial
   sweetener

2 large oranges

25 g (1 oz) plain chocolate

NUTRITION

Each portion contains:

Energy: 165 calories

Fat: 4 g of which saturates 2 g

1 Dissolve the jelly crystals in 140 ml (¼ pint) boiling water and set aside to cool completely.

2 Place the fromage frais in a bowl and sieve in the cocoa powder. In another bowl whisk the egg whites until stiff.

3 Whisk the cooled jelly into the fromage frais and add sufficient sweetener to taste. Fold in the egg whites and either spoon into four serving dishes or one large dish. Chill for 1–2 hours or until set.

4 Meanwhile, slice the top and bottom off each orange and slice off the peel, taking away as much of the white pith as possible. Slice in between each segment to release the flesh. Cover and chill until required.

5 To serve, arrange a few slices of orange on top of each mousse and grate over the chocolate.

COOK'S TIP

Please note that the government advises that the elderly, babies and pregnant women should not eat raw eggs.

TIRAMISU

SERVES 6   PREPARATION AND COOKING: 20 MINS, PLUS CHILLING

INGREDIENTS

2 medium egg yolks

3 tbsp granulated artificial
    sweetener

few drops vanilla essence to taste

400 g (14 oz) low-fat soft cheese

12 sponge fingers

2 tsp instant coffee dissolved in
    2 tbsp water

2 tbsp brandy

145 g (5 oz) very low-fat fromage
    frais

12 chocolate-covered coffee beans

2 level tsp cocoa powder

NUTRITION

Each portion contains:

Energy: 170 calories

Fat: 4 g of which saturates 1.5 g

1 In a mixing bowl, whisk together the egg yolks and 2 tbsp sweetener until thick and creamy. Add the vanilla essence and 2 tbsp cheese and whisk in gently. Gradually whisk in the remaining cheese to form a smooth cream.

2 Break the sponge fingers in half and place them in a shallow dish. Mix the coffee and brandy together and drizzle over the sponge fingers, mixing them gently to coat them in the liquid.

3 Divide half the sponge fingers between six small serving glasses. Top with half the cream mixture, then with the rest of the sponge fingers and a second layer of cream. Chill for 30 minutes.

4 To serve, sweeten the fromage frais with the remaining sweetener and spoon on top of each glass. Decorate with the coffee beans and dust with the cocoa.

COOK'S TIP

So, you think tiramisu is off the menu when you're losing weight? Think again! With a few simple low-fat switches, our slimline version of this classic Italian dessert looks and tastes sensational. Please note that the government advises that the elderly, babies and pregnant women should not eat raw eggs.

CHUNKY BREAD PUDDING

SERVES: 6   PREPARATION: 10 MINS, PLUS STANDING

COOKING: 40 MINS

INGREDIENTS

4 x 55 g (2 oz) soft wholemeal
   bread rolls
55 g (2 oz) sultanas
6 medium eggs
500 g (1 lb 2 oz) very low-fat
   fromage frais
1 tsp ground mixed spice
2–3 tbsp granulated artificial
   sweetener

NUTRITION

Each portion contains:

Energy: 250 calories

Fat: 8 g of which saturates 2 g

1 Preheat the oven to 180°C/350°F/Gas 4. Cut the bread rolls into small cubes and place in a shallow ovenproof gratin dish. Sprinkle over the sultanas.

2 Beat the eggs together and mix into the fromage frais to form a custard. Add the spice and sufficient sweetener to taste.

3 Spoon the fromage frais custard over the bread and turn the bread over in the custard to make sure it is completely covered.

4 Stand the dish in a roasting tin and pour sufficient boiling water into the tin to come halfway up the sides of the gratin dish. Bake in the oven for 35–40 minutes until set and a knife inserted in the centre comes out clean.

5 Remove the dish from the tin and stand for 10 minutes before serving, sprinkled with extra sweetener if liked.

COOK'S TIP

You could also make this recipe using the same weight of soft wholemeal bread. Cut the loaf into thick slices, then into small cubes.

PEAR AND RASPBERRY CRISP

SERVES: 4   PREPARATION: 15 MINS   COOKING: 12 MINS

INGREDIENTS

4 ripe pears

juice and rind of 1 lemon

225 g (8 oz) raspberries, thawed
  if frozen

2–3 tsp granulated artificial
  sweetener

40 g (1½ oz) cornflakes

4 level tsp maple syrup

25 g (1 oz) low-fat spread

NUTRITION

Each portion contains:

Energy: 150 calories

Fat: 3 g of which saturates 1 g

1 Core and peel the pears. Cut into thick wedges and place in a large saucepan. Tip the lemon rind into the saucepan and add the lemon juice. Mix the pears in the juice until well coated.

2 Pour in 145 ml (¼ pint) water. Bring to the boil, cover and simmer for 5 minutes. If using fresh raspberries, wash them. Add the raspberries to the saucepan and mix together gently. Continue to cook, covered, for a further 2–3 minutes or until tender. Add sweetener to taste, then transfer the fruit to a shallow ovenproof dish.

3 Place the cornflakes in a mixing bowl. Place the maple syrup and low-fat spread in a small saucepan and melt over a very low heat. Toss into the cornflakes and stir until they are well coated. Scatter the cornflakes on top of the fruit to lightly cover it.

4 Preheat the grill to a hot setting and cook the fruit crisp for 1–2 minutes or until the topping is bubbling and lightly golden.

COOK'S TIP

This crunchy topping livens up lightly cooked fruit to make a colourful and very delicious pudding. It is also good made with blackberries and apple (use equal quantities of each).

STRAWBERRY AND RASPBERRY FILO SLICES

SERVES: 4   PREPARATION: 20 MINS, PLUS COOLING

COOKING: 10 MINS

INGREDIENTS

3 x 25 g (1 oz) large sheets frozen
    filo pastry, thawed

1 medium egg, beaten

115 g (4 oz) small strawberries

115 g (4 oz) raspberries, thawed if
    frozen

285 g (10 oz) very low-fat fromage
    frais

1 tsp almond essence

1–2 tbsp granulated artificial
    sweetener

2 level tsp icing sugar

mint to decorate

NUTRITION

Each portion contains:

Energy: 155 calories

Fat: 2.5 g of which saturates 0.5 g

1 Preheat the oven to 200°C/400°F/Gas 6. Lay the sheets of filo on the work surface and brush with beaten egg. Fold over lengthwise, brush with more egg and fold again to make three long strips.

2 Cut the strips into four equal portions and lay side by side on a baking sheet lined with baking parchment. Brush with more egg and bake for 8–10 minutes or until golden brown. Carefully remove the pastry portions from the paper and allow them to cool on a wire rack.

3 Meanwhile, wash, hull and halve the strawberries. If using fresh raspberries, wash them. Mix together the strawberries and raspberries, cover and chill. Mix the fromage frais with the almond essence and sufficient sweetener to taste. Cover and chill until required.

4 To serve, place a piece of crisp pastry on each of four serving plates. Cover with half the fromage frais and fruit. Lay another sheet on top and repeat with the rest of the fromage frais and fruit. Finally place the remaining pastry on top, dust with icing sugar and decorate with mint. Serve immediately.

COOK'S TIP

These pastries are best served as soon as they are assembled, otherwise the pastry may soften.